Autumn Leaves

by
Gail Saunder

Pebble Books

an imprint of Capstone Press

Pebble Books are published by Capstone Press
151 Good Counsel Drive, P.O. Box 669, Mankato, Minnesota 56002
www.capstonepub.com

 Books published by Capstone Press are manufactured with paper
containing at least 10 percent post-consumer waste.

Library of Congress Cataloging-in-Publication Data
Saunders-Smith, Gail.
  Autumn leaves/ by Gail Saunders-Smith.
    p. cm.
  Includes bibliographical references (p. 23) and index.
  Summary: Simple text and photographs present the different types and colors of
leaves found in the Northern Hemisphere in autumn.
  ISBN-13: 978-1-56065-586-2 (hardcover)   ISBN-10: 1-56065-586-0 (hardcover)
  ISBN-13: 978-1-56065-958-7 (softcover)   ISBN-10: 1-56065-958-0 (softcover)
  1. Leaves—Color—Juvenile literature. 2. Fall foliage—Juvenile literature.
[1. Leaves. 2. Fall foliage.] I. Title
QK649.S26 1998   97-29801
581.4'8—dc21   CIP
                                                              AC

Editorial Credits
Lois Wallentine, editor; Timothy Halldin and James Franklin, design; Michelle L.
Norstad, photo research

Photo Credits
William D. Adams, 10
Barbara Comnes, 1, 12
John Dittli, 14
Cheryl A. Ertlet, 6
International Stock/Hardie Truesdale, 18; Chuck Szymanski, 20
Cheryl Richter, 8
Mark Turner, 4, 16
Unicorn Stock/Chromosohm/Sohm, cover

Printed in the United States of America in North Mankato, Minnesota.
112010
005998R

Table of Contents

4

green leaves

red leaves

yellow leaves

orange leaves

gold   leaves

brown   leaves

dead leaves

no leaves

winter

Words to Know

dead—no longer alive

leaves—the flat and usually green parts of a tree; leaves sometimes change colors during fall.

winter—the season between fall and spring; the weather is at its coldest.

Read More

Gamlin, Linda. *Trees.* Eyewitness Explorers. New York: Dorling Kindersley, 1993.

Johnson, Sylvia A. *How Leaves Change* Minneapolis: Lerner Publishing Company, 1986.

Pluckrose, Henry Arthur. *Trees.* Chicago: Children's Press, 1994.

Internet Sites

FactHound offers a safe, fun way to find Internet sites related to this book.

Go to *www.facthound.com*

He'll fetch the best sites for you!

Note to Parents and Teachers

This caption book illustrates different colors of leaves found in autumn. The clear photographs support the beginning reader in making and maintaining the meaning of the simple text. The noun repeats on each page while the adjective changes. The structure changes on the last page where the noun changes. All changes are depicted in the photographs. Children may need assistance in using the Table of Contents, Words to Know, Read More, Internet Sites, and Index/Word List sections of the book.

Index/Word List

Word Count: 17
Early-Intervention Level: 2